Colin POWELL

Biography

Colin POWELL

Reggie Finlayson

Lerner Publications Company
Minneapolis

To my parents, William and Edith Finlayson,
who have always seemed heroic to me

This book is available in two editions:
Library binding by Lerner Publications Company,
  a division of Lerner Publishing Group
Soft cover by First Avenue Editions,
  an imprint of Lerner Publishing Group
241 First Avenue North
Minneapolis, MN 55401 U.S.A.

Website addresses: www.lernerbooks.com
                www.biography.com

Library of Congress Cataloging-in-Publication Data

Finlayson, Reggie.
    Colin Powell / by Reggie Finlayson.
      p.   cm. — (A&E biography)
    Includes bibliographical references and index.
    Summary: A biography covering the childhood and military and political careers of General Colin Powell.
    ISBN: 0–8225–4966–2 (lib. bdg. : alk. paper)
    ISBN: 0–8225–9698–9 (pbk. : alk. paper)
    1. Powell, Colin L.—Juvenile literature. 2. Statesmen—United States—Biography—Juvenile literature. 3. Generals—United States—Biography—Juvenile literature. 4. African American generals—Biography—Juvenile literature. 5. United States. Army—Biography—Juvenile literature. [1. Powell, Colin L. 2. Cabinet officers. 3. Generals. 4. African Americans—Biography.] I. Title. II. Biography (Lerner Publications Company). III. Series.
    E840.8.P64F56 2004
    327.73'092—dc21   2002156556

Manufactured in the United States of America
1 2 3 4 5 6 – JR – 09 08 07 06 05 04

CONTENTS

Colin Powell grew up in New York City's bustling South Bronx neighborhood.

INTRODUCTION: ORDINARY OR EXTRAORDINARY?

It was the summer of 1950. Thirteen-year-old Colin Powell, the son of Jamaican immigrants, had received a special honor. His family's priest, Father Weeden, had chosen Colin to attend a church camp near Peekskill, New York. There were just a few openings at the camp, so the selection was an honor and a source of pride for Colin and his parents.

Besides that, the camp offered an inviting change of pace from Colin's day-to-day life. He lived in the South Bronx—a loud, bustling, diverse neighborhood in New York City. The streets there were lined with old apartment houses and family-owned shops. Colin and his friends usually spent their summers playing in the streets, amid the crowded brick buildings and sounds of honking car horns. Colin was black, as were many of his friends. But other friends were Puerto Rican, Jewish, Italian, and Hungarian. Many neighborhood families, like Colin's, had immigrated to the United States earlier in the century.

WHO WILL OWN UP LIKE A MAN?

The summer camp was about an hour's drive north of New York in a quiet country setting. Colin was excited to leave New York City for the green, woodsy camp.

But shortly after arriving, he fell in with a bad group of boys. One night the boys smuggled beer into the camp. They didn't think anyone had seen them as they returned with all the stealth of Army Rangers. They confidently hid the cans of beer in a toilet tank to cool. Then they returned to the other campers.

The boys thought they were home free and felt triumphant as they mingled with the other campers. Each wore a smile of satisfaction, thinking they had a winning plan. But they weren't as smart as they thought. It wasn't long before the priest in charge found the beer and summoned all the campers to the meeting hall.

He surveyed the young audience coolly before announcing his discovery. Backs stiffened throughout the hall as the boys considered the harsh discipline likely to flow from this incident. They silently braced themselves for the expected storm of words. But the priest didn't threaten. He didn't even preach. He spoke in a quiet, firm voice: "Who will own up like a man?" he asked. The words hung in the air like breath on a cold day.

Was that it? Colin wondered. The possibilities flashed in his mind. He was sure no one had seen them. No one else knew who was guilty. All the boys had to do was keep quiet. Colin certainly didn't want to suffer the shame of getting caught. More than that, he had no wish to suffer his father's disapproval.

Summer camp offered a refreshing change for city boys like Colin.

Just keep quiet, he thought to himself. But even as he thought it, the priest's words echoed in his mind with increasing volume. Who will own up like a man? Who will own up like a man? Suddenly, things seemed very clear for Colin. Without further hesitation, he rose and said: "Father, I did it." Then, two other boys surprised him. They stood to admit their part in the deed, refusing to let him take the blame alone.

Justice was swift. The priest put the humiliated boys on the next train back to New York City. It was a long and sad journey. But the worst part for Colin was the walk to his house at 952 Kelly Street. The buildings seemed to press in on him. His shoulders ached. But that was just the beginning.

Bad news travels fast, and Colin's disgrace was on everyone's lips when he entered the family home. His mother, Arie Powell, spoke first. Her sharp questions cut deeper with each pass. Then his father, Luther Powell, joined in with his own angry words. Colin could not help feeling ashamed. It seemed like he would carry the mark of a hoodlum or thug from that time forward.

Just then the telephone rang. It was Father Weeden calling for Mr. Powell. Colin watched as his father's grim face softened and even became friendly. He saw

Colin's father, Luther Powell, was disappointed in Colin's behavior at summer camp. But he was impressed by Colin's integrity and honesty.

a reaction that gave him hope. Later, his father repeated the priest's words. It was true that the boys had behaved badly, Father Weeden said. "But your Colin stood up and took responsibility. And his example spurred the other boys to admit their guilt." His parents beamed. They were again proud of their son. Colin had not only shown integrity, but he also seemed to bring that trait out in others. He was, according to his father and mother, a real Powell.

Years later, as an adult, Colin Powell often recalled the incident. Sometimes it made him laugh to remember his mistake. Other times he thought about the mark the event had left on him. He had learned about honesty that summer. Honesty wasn't just something he talked about after that. It was something he tried to live by.

AN AMERICAN JOURNEY

Young Colin Powell was not an exceptional student or an exceptional athlete. For many years, he showed no signs of greatness. He was a black child from an immigrant family, growing up during a time when blacks in the United States were often viewed as second-class citizens. His family did not have much money. They could not send him to fancy schools. Few people expected Colin Powell to do anything out of the ordinary.

But inside this seemingly average young man, there were qualities—such as the honesty, integrity, and courage that he had demonstrated at summer camp—that would make young Powell a great leader one day.

Secretary of State Colin Powell, left, *President George W. Bush,* center, *and Secretary of Defense Donald Rumsfeld,* right, *listen attentively during a meeting on international affairs.*

Eventually, the whole world would see those traits very clearly.

By the early twenty-first century, Colin Powell was anything but ordinary. In the half century since his unexceptional childhood, he had risen through the ranks of the military and government. Finally he held one of the most important jobs in the world: secretary of state of the United States of America. In this position, Powell represented the United States to all the nations of the globe. The U.S. president relied on Powell's opinions when making crucial decisions on international affairs. Other world leaders clamored to meet with him. They paid careful attention to his words and ideas. They knew that his views and his opinions could change the course of history.

How did Colin Powell, a boy from the gritty South Bronx streets, become one of the most powerful people in the world? How did he become one of the most admired and respected Americans in public life? What is his story? In his autobiography, *My American Journey*, Colin Powell answers the questions this way: "[Mine] is a story of hard work and good luck, of occasional rough times. . . . It is a story of faith—faith in myself, and faith in America. Above all, it's a love story: love of family, of friends, of the Army, and of my country. It is a story that could only have happened in America."

Immigrants stream from the processing center at New York's Ellis Island in the 1920s. Powell's parents were among the many newcomers who sought better lives in the United States.

Chapter **ONE**

THE STREETS
OF NEW YORK

IN THE EARLY TWENTIETH CENTURY, NEW YORK CITY drew people like a magnet. Writers, musicians, and artists came to take part in the city's rich cultural life. Laborers and entrepreneurs came for jobs and business opportunities. Immigrants flooded in from all over the world, seeking employment, education, and religious freedom. African Americans flocked to New York, too. They came to find jobs and schooling. And they came to live free of the prejudice and discrimination that frequently plagued their lives in other parts of the United States, especially the American South.

In the 1920s, Luther Powell and Maud Ariel "Arie" McKoy joined the flood of newcomers into New York City.

Luther and Arie came from Jamaica, an island in the Caribbean Sea, part of a group of islands called the West Indies. They had grown up near one another on Jamaica, both in farming families, but they had not known each other there. They arrived in New York separately but chased the same dream—the dream of a better life in the United States.

Although the exact dates and details aren't certain, sometime in the 1920s Arie McKoy arrived in New York. She came to join her mother, Alice, and a large clan of McKoys who had already settled in the United States. She came armed with a high school diploma and experience working in a lawyer's office. In New York, she found a job as a seamstress. She worked at home, sewing buttons and trim on clothing. She was paid by the piece—the more garments she finished, the more money she made.

Luther Powell had also attended high school in Jamaica. But he hadn't graduated. Instead, he took a job in a store, but it didn't offer many opportunities or rewards. So he packed up and moved. He boarded a United Fruit Company steamer, a boat filled with bananas that was bound for Philadelphia, Pennsylvania. When he stepped off the boat, he had little more than the clothes he was wearing. But he was confident that with a fair chance, he could stand toe-to-toe with anybody in the United States.

Luther was the first of his family members to move to the United States. Eventually, many of his brothers, sisters, and cousins would also arrive from Jamaica. Luther first worked as a gardener on estates in Connecticut, then as a building manager in Manhattan. Finally, he went to work in Manhattan's garment district, beginning in the stockroom of Ginsburg's, a clothing manufacturer.

Luther met Arie McKoy at her mother's home, where he rented a room for a time. Their relationship blossomed, and they were married on December 28, 1929.

Arie McKoy, about the time she married Luther Powell

They settled into a brick apartment house on Morningside Avenue in a part of New York called Harlem. This neighborhood was home to thousands of West Indian immigrants like the Powells, as well as U.S.-born African Americans. The Powells' first child, Marilyn, was born in Harlem in 1931. Their second child, Colin Luther Powell, was born about five and a half years later, on April 5, 1937.

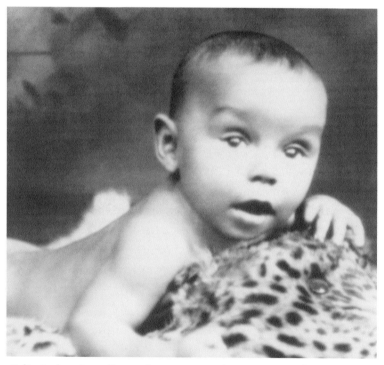

Colin Luther Powell was born on April 5, 1937. Colin was the Powells' second child.

How Do You Pronounce "Colin"?

olin Powell pronounces his name KOH-lihn instead of the usual KAH-lihn. Where did that pronunciation come from? Actually, Colin's family used the KAH-lihn pronunciation from the start. Then bomber pilot Colin Kelly Jr. became famous for his heroism in World War II (1939–1945). His name was pronounced KOH-lihn, and Colin's friends often heard the name on the radio. They began to use Kelly's pronunciation to refer to their friend Colin Powell. Although his family continued to call him KAH-lihn, the KOH-lihn pronunciation stuck.

THE JAMAICAN GODFATHER

Colin Powell's life began at the tail end of the Great Depression, an era of business failures, hunger, and widespread unemployment in the United States. Times were hard everywhere in those days, especially in the African American community. The Powells were not a wealthy family, but they were luckier than most. They had a place to live, food to eat, and a steady income.

Luther and Arie wanted the best for their two children. They worked hard and set money aside. At Ginsburg's (later named the Gaines Company), Luther earned a series of promotions. After starting in the stockroom, he eventually became foreman of the company's shipping department.

Gradually, more and more Powell relatives arrived in New York from Jamaica. Luther quickly became the leader of this growing clan. When there was trouble, relatives asked for his advice or financial support. "His take-charge manner was reassuring," Colin wrote in his autobiography many years later. "Luther Powell became the Godfather, the one people came to for advice . . . for help in getting a job."

When Colin was four years old, the family left Harlem for the Hunts Point section of the South Bronx. The move marked a step up for the Powells. By then their Harlem neighborhood had grown rundown and dangerous. The South Bronx, by comparison, was clean and safe. It was home to a variety of working-class people from many ethnic and religious backgrounds.

The Powells moved into a four-bedroom home in a four-story brick apartment house on Kelly Street. Many of their relatives lived just down the street or around the corner. Colin grew up listening to the lilting West Indian accents of his aunts and uncles, and his grandmother Alice McKoy, along with their fond stories of childhood in Jamaica. Luther Powell was especially social. It was not uncommon for him to invite the mailman, the garbageman, or the oilman up to the house for coffee.

IMAGES OF WAR

In many ways, Colin's childhood was typical. Like many boys his age, he enjoyed games such as stickball, marbles, and capture the flag. He loved riding his bike down Kelly Street, flying kites from the roofs of neighborhood buildings, and watching cowboy movies at the Tiffany Theater on Saturdays. His family was active in St. Margaret's Episcopal Church, and Colin became an acolyte, or assistant to the priest, there.

But Colin grew up during the early 1940s, and these were not ordinary years in the United States. Starting in 1939, World War II raged in Europe. Two years later the United States joined the Allies in fighting Germany, Italy, and Japan. Millions of young men shipped out for combat, while Americans left at home pitched in to help the war effort.

For young Colin, only four when the United States entered the fighting, the war seemed exciting. Through newspapers, newsreels shown at the movies, and radio broadcasts, he and his friends learned about heroic American soldiers. One was Audie Murphy, an army lieutenant who single-handedly killed about fifty German troops in one battle. Another was Colin Kelly Jr., a pilot who was shot down after bombing a Japanese warship.

The boys directed mock battles on the living room floor, complete with toy soldiers, model airplanes, and tissue-paper parachutes. "My pals and I scanned the skies from the rooftops looking for Messerschmitts or Heinkels [German aircraft] that might get through to bomb Hunts Point," Colin remembers. "We sprayed imaginary enemies with imaginary weapons."[4] Colin was "always in love with the Army," remarked a friend.

Young Powell and his friends admired American heroes of World War II. One group of aviators (called the Tuskegee Airmen) were the first black American combat pilots.

"We grew up at the end of World War II. It was when we became aware of the world and of life."

Colin attended P.S. 39, the local elementary school. He was put in a class for slow learners, which disappointed his parents. His sister, Marilyn, was an excellent student, so Colin just looked worse by comparison. He attended P.S. 52, a rough all-boys school, for junior high, followed by four years at Morris High School. Although his attendance was good and he kept up with his homework, he still lagged behind his sister and many other students in his class. He earned a C average during his high school career.

Though not a great student, Colin was nevertheless industrious. He remained active at St. Margaret's Church. He loved his job as an acolyte and later as a subdeacon, a position that held significant responsibility. He greatly admired the church's pageantry, organization, and tradition. After school and on weekends, Colin worked unloading trucks, shipping packages, and assembling baby furniture at a store called Sickser's. The store's Jewish owners and customers even taught Colin a few words of Yiddish, a language that Jewish immigrants to the United States had brought over with them from Europe.

In 1954 Colin took a summer job at a soft drink bottling plant. The pay was ninety cents an hour, more than he made at Sickser's. Colin eyed with enthusiasm the workers who tended the plant's high-tech bottling equipment and conveyor belts. That was the job he wanted. But there was one catch. Colin was black. The plant managers allowed only white employees to operate the bottling machines. The foreman put Colin to work mopping floors.

Colin had grown up in a neighborhood crowded with minorities—blacks and Puerto Ricans, Jews, Poles, Greeks, Hungarians, and Italians. Since everyone was a minority, no one ethnic group was regularly singled out for discrimination. The restrictions at the soft drink plant gave Colin one of his first tastes of racial injustice. Eventually, though, the managers relaxed the rules and let Colin work on the bottling machines.

Colin Powell, about the time he graduated from high school.
His parents encouraged Powell to go on to college.

Chapter **TWO**

SOLDIERING ON

AFTER COLIN'S LACKLUSTER PERFORMANCE IN HIGH school, his parents had reason for concern. Luther and Arie Powell had not gone past high school themselves. They were working-class people who made a living with their hands. Still, they valued education, as did most of their Jamaican relatives in the United States. There was no question in their minds that Colin should go to college. Arie had a very specific idea about her son's career path. "You got to go in engineering; that's where the money is, man,"[6] she told her son.

Colin wanted to please his parents. After all, they had sacrificed to make his life better. What could he do but try? So he applied to New York University

(NYU) and the City College of New York (CCNY), both located in Manhattan. Despite his C average in high school, both schools accepted him.

It was easy to decide between them. The tuition at NYU was $750 a year but only $10 a year at CCNY. So CCNY it was. It was a college for the children of working-class parents. It was inexpensive but not inferior. Its graduates—including research scientist Jonas Salk, labor leader A. Philip Randolph, and writer Upton Sinclair—were among the best and the brightest in the world.

Colin started classes at CCNY in the winter of 1954. He lived at home with his parents, riding the bus to and from campus. At his mother's suggestion, he set out to study engineering. But he quickly found that he didn't do well in the science and math courses required for that program. He did enjoy geology, though, and eventually majored in that field. As he later explained to his parents, with a geology degree, he could get a job with an oil company.

A MAN IN UNIFORM

Early on at CCNY, Colin noticed a number of young men who stood out because of the uniforms they wore. They belonged to the Reserve Officers Training Corps (ROTC), an educational program for military officers. The ROTC operated at schools and colleges across the United States, with separate programs for the army, navy, and air force. CCNY had fifteen

Powell excelled in the Army ROTC program at the City College of New York. He is shown here at the rank of sergeant first class.

hundred ROTC cadets, the largest group in the United States. Colin had been captivated by the military since his boyhood during World War II. He was immediately drawn to the corps, and he joined Army ROTC in the fall of 1954.

Colin quickly came to love everything about the program. He looked forward to the drills and the military education. He soon joined a military fraternity called the Pershing Rifles—a group that seemed to take soldiering more seriously than the other ROTC cadets.

"For the first time in my life I was a member of a brotherhood," Powell would later say about the Pershing Rifles. "The discipline, the structure, the camaraderie, the sense of belonging were what I craved. . . . I found a selflessness within our ranks that reminded me of the caring atmosphere within my family. Race, color, background, income meant nothing."

Colin quickly became a leader in the Pershing Rifles. In his junior year, he took charge of recruiting the group's new members, and he eventually became its company commander. One of his closest friends in the group was Tony Mavroudis, a Greek American who was set on a career in the military. He and Colin became extremely close—almost like brothers. They visited with one another's parents, double-dated, and hit the town after class.

Meanwhile, Colin limped along in school, once again earning Cs in most of his academic classes. But in his ROTC coursework—map reading, infantry tactics, marksmanship—Powell was a top student. That work kept him engaged and pushed him forward. "I really don't know if I would have finished college if it had not been for the ROTC program," Colin later told a reporter.

Colin graduated from CCNY in June 1958 with a bachelor's degree in geology. But he also held something far more important: with his completion of the CCNY ROTC program, Powell had become a second lieutenant, a commissioned officer, in the U.S. Army.

COMMISSIONED OFFICERS IN THE U.S. ARMY

Colin Powell served as a commissioned officer in the U.S. Army. Commissioned officers are the highest-ranking officers in the army. They generally receive their training through ROTC, the United States Military Academy, or another specialized school. Other kinds of army officers are called noncommissioned officers and warrant officers. Both groups are generally enlisted personnel who become officers by mastering special skills or showing exceptional leadership abilities. The following are the commissioned ranks for the U.S. Army from lowest (top left) to highest (bottom right):

- Second lieutenant
- First lieutenant
- Captain
- Major
- Lieutenant colonel
- Colonel

- Brigadier general (1 star)
- Major general (2 stars)
- Lieutenant general (3 stars)
- General (4 stars)
- General of the Army (5 stars, wartime only)

At last, the ordinary boy with the average grades had found his calling. He had become a soldier.

LEARNING THE BASICS

Two days after graduation, Colin Powell boarded a bus and headed south. His destination was Fort Benning, Georgia, and the Infantry Officers Basic Course.

That was where new lieutenants were trained in the basics of frontline fighting: survival skills, hand-to-hand combat, and handling prisoners of war. It was a grueling two-month program, but more difficult training followed.

Powell signed on for two specialized schools, which would qualify him to serve in the army's most elite fighting units. First came Ranger school, extreme training for foot soldiers. There, Powell and the other students waded through snake-filled swamps, scaled cliffs, and marched all night long with fifty-pound packs and machine guns slung over their shoulders.

Next, he enrolled in the army's airborne program, which trained him to be a paratrooper. After the first few weeks spent rappelling off cliffs and parachuting off towers, the men boarded a twin-engine C-123 transport plane for the real thing—a parachute jump from several thousand feet up. "I felt a cold anxiety as I stood in the door of the plane . . . ," Powell recalled. "Jumping into nothingness goes against our deepest human instincts. Nevertheless, I made five jumps in two days."

Powell stayed at Fort Benning for about five months. During this time, he earned the widespread respect of the other young officers there. He stood out for his intelligence, leadership, and positive attitude. "Sometimes when things got going a little tough, Colin Powell was the one that would rise above it," recalls William Roosma, a friend from Fort Benning. "He always had a smile, a sense of humor to bring things back in perspective again. . . . He had a sense of confidence about himself that was like an aura. He truly had so much self-confidence."

On the base, Powell was "one of the guys"—one of a cocky group of Rangers who were eager to get into the field and do some real fighting. Off base, however, was another story. Because Powell was black, the bars outside Fort Benning wouldn't serve him when he and his friends went there to relax at night. Fort Benning was in the heart of the Old South. Segregation—the strict separation of blacks and whites—was the rule there.

Although Fort Benning was desegregated, Powell found that the separation of blacks and whites was fully enforced off the base.

At first, Powell's friends protested on his behalf. They even started a few brawls in the bars that refused to serve him. But eventually Powell just avoided the embarrassment. When his friends went out at night, he stayed home by himself, claiming he was too busy to leave the base.

COLD COLD WAR

By then there was little doubt that Colin Powell would make his career in the army. For his first official job, he was assigned to a base in Gelnhausen, West Germany, as a platoon leader in charge of more than forty men. The base occupied a strategic position in the mountains, designed to hold off a potential attack by a feared U.S. enemy—the powerful Soviet Union (USSR). At the time, the United States and the Soviets were engaged in the bitter Cold War—a hostile period from about 1945 to 1991 marked by rivalry and mistrust between the two nations but with no real fighting.

In Germany Powell and his men spent most of their time sitting outside in frigid vehicles, scanning the skies for a Soviet attack that never came. Though he saw no action, the soldier's life clearly suited Lieutenant Powell. He loved the discipline and the sense of fellowship among the troops. He loved learning about a foreign country. He was respected and well liked by the other soldiers, and he did his job well. In late 1959, he was promoted to first lieutenant—his first step up the military ladder. His two-year service in Germany even included a celebrity encounter. In late 1960, he met the famous rock-and-roll singer Elvis Presley, who had been drafted into the army a few years earlier.

What Powell disliked about his time in Germany was the loneliness. He had been raised in a lively home, where people joked and laughed, grieved and cried with gusto. He missed his family and was happy when he was transferred back to the United States in 1960.

MAKING TIME FOR LOVE

This time he was stationed at Fort Devens, Massachusetts, assigned to command a company, a job usually held by a captain, not a lieutenant. The assignment had its perks. New York was only a few hours away. Powell could easily go there on his days off. He looked forward to plenty of visits and lots of home cooking.

One weekend, a fellow officer named Michael Heningburg asked Colin a question. Heningburg dated a woman in Boston, and she had a roommate, Alma Johnson. Would Colin like to meet Alma and accompany Heningburg and his girlfriend on a double date? The young lieutenant was not optimistic about blind dates. He agreed to accompany his friend, but he didn't have high hopes.

Twenty-four-year-old Alma Johnson, a graduate student at Boston's Emerson College, was not crazy about blind dates either. And she was especially wary of soldiers. The romantic possibilities didn't seem promising.

Alma and Colin, however, were pleasantly surprised upon meeting. Alma liked Colin's baby face and easy-going manner. To Colin, Alma was simply unforgettable.

A southerner, born and raised in Birmingham, Alabama, Alma was graceful, intelligent, and kind. She had soft green eyes, brown hair, and a slim build. Alma had studied at Fisk University, one of the nation's best all-black colleges. In Boston she studied audiology, a field that involves working with hearing-impaired people.

After their first date, Colin and Alma saw a lot of each other. The relationship grew serious, but there was no talk of marriage. In August 1962, Colin received new orders from the army. He was first to report to Fort Bragg, North Carolina, for specialized training. A promotion to captain would follow. After that he was on his way overseas again, for a one-year assignment in a small, little-known country in Southeast Asia. Its name was South Vietnam.

When Alma heard that Colin was leaving the country, she suggested that they end their relationship. Who knew what the next year would bring? Alma didn't want to sit and wait for Colin, with no guarantee they'd be together when he returned.

That settled it—Colin decided to offer Alma a guarantee. He proposed marriage—and he wanted to do it fast, before his next assignment got in the way of their plans. Arrangements were made practically overnight. Colin asked his commanding officer for a

*Colin Powell and
Alma Johnson on their
wedding day, August
25, 1962*

weekend off. Two weeks after the proposal, on August 25, 1962, Colin Powell and Alma Johnson were married on a hot day in Birmingham, Alabama.

The young couple took an apartment in Boston. But it was just temporary. After a few months, Colin moved to Fort Bragg for a five-week training session at the army's Unconventional Warfare Center. Alma moved with him, but they both knew that their time together would be short. Just before Christmas, orders came down for Powell to report for duty in Vietnam.

Early in his military career, First Lieutenant Powell was assigned to serve in South Vietnam.

Chapter **THREE**

OVER WHERE?

ALTHOUGH **POWELL HAD KNOWN IN ADVANCE** about his Vietnam assignment, his family members were confused when they heard the news. Like most Americans, they had never heard of the small country on the other side of the world.

But though it was small and far away, Vietnam was of great military concern to the U.S. government. The country had been a French colony in the late nineteenth century and early twentieth century. Then, a group of communist fighters forced the French out. Communism—a system in which the government controls the economy, with no private property—was deeply worrisome to the United States. Most Americans saw communism as a potential threat to freedom and democracy.

The Soviet Union was a communist nation, as was China, located directly north of Vietnam. The United States wanted to make sure that Vietnam and other nations didn't fall under communist control.

At an international peace conference in 1954, Vietnam was divided into two parts: communist North Vietnam, with close ties to the Soviet Union; and noncommunist South Vietnam, supported by the United States and its allies. Despite this agreement, many people in both North and South Vietnam wanted communism extended into the South. Warfare broke out between communist fighters and the South Vietnamese government.

That's where Colin Powell came in. He was part of a force of more than eleven thousand American troops stationed in Vietnam in the early years of the 1960s. They were not fighting troops but rather advisers to the South Vietnamese. Their job was to help South Vietnamese soldiers resist a communist takeover. Young Powell had half hoped for an assignment like this. Finally, there'd be an opportunity for some real soldiering.

The order was bittersweet. He would depart for Vietnam two days before Christmas. That alone was enough to take the joy out of the holiday. But there was more. Alma was pregnant, and Colin's yearlong tour of duty meant that he would miss the birth of their first child. The Powells also had the unspoken dread shared by every military family—that their soldier might die in combat.

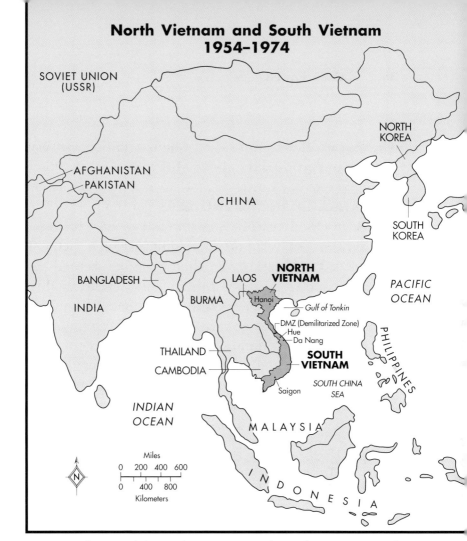

North Vietnam and South Vietnam 1954–1974

SOVIET UNION
(USSR)

NORTH KOREA

AFGHANISTAN
PAKISTAN

CHINA

SOUTH KOREA

BANGLADESH

LAOS

NORTH VIETNAM

PACIFIC OCEAN

INDIA

BURMA

Hanoi

Gulf of Tonkin

DMZ (Demilitarized Zone)
Hue
Da Nang

THAILAND

SOUTH VIETNAM

CAMBODIA

Saigon

SOUTH CHINA SEA

PHILIPPINES

INDIAN OCEAN

MALAYSIA

Miles
0   200   400   600

0   400   800
Kilometers

N

INDONESIA

Hoping to bring stability to the region, members of an international conference voted to divide Vietnam in 1954.

   Alma knew she would spend many nights worrying about Colin and missing him. But she bore the situation with stoic calm. The orders brought the reality of military life into sharp focus, and she accepted the complications. If Colin was going to make a mark in the military, he would need the support of his family.

Alma was willing to give that. She would live with her parents in Birmingham during his tour.

NIGHTMARE IN PARADISE

Colin arrived in Saigon, South Vietnam, on Christmas morning in 1962. The country was lush and green, a land of rice farmers and fishermen that seemed too peaceful and lovely to be a battlefield. The landscape looked like a picture in a travel brochure. But unseen forces were at work—forces that would make this tropical paradise a nightmare of war for years to come.

Saigon was the capital of South Vietnam. A port city, located at the southern tip of a landmass jutting into the

Citizens of Saigon go about their day in 1962. Powell arrived in the capital city on Christmas Day of that year.

Powell was stationed at A Shau, above, in 1962. The strategic base overlooked the A Shau Valley and the Ho Chi Minh Trail.

South China Sea, it teemed with people hustling about on foot and in pedal-driven cabs called cyclos. Fine restaurants and expensive shops filled the city. Fashionable women dressed in silk strolled gracefully along the streets. Because the city was so elegant and had absorbed French influence during colonization, it had been dubbed "the Paris of the Orient."

Powell took in the sights, smells, and sounds of the place for a few days. Within a week, he headed north to a base called A Shau, located in a tropical forest along the western border with Laos. He was there to advise a South Vietnamese unit led by Captain Vo Cong Hieu that was stationed at the base. The base sat in a valley along the Ho Chi Minh Trail.

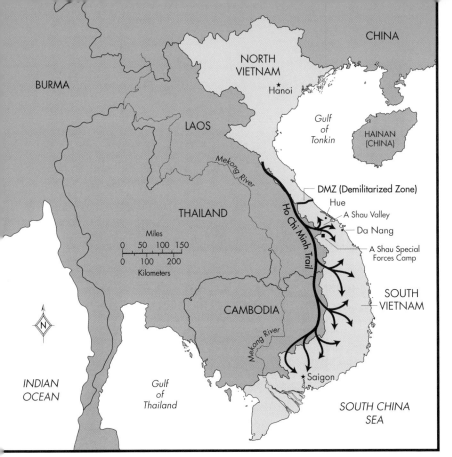

The Ho Chi Minh Trail between North Vietnam and South Vietnam

The trail was a vital North Vietnamese supply route named after the country's leader. The unit's mission was to slow the flow of men and supplies moving along the trail to communist fighters in the South.

The countryside surrounding A Shau was beautiful but extremely rugged. Powell knew that it would test every bit of a soldier's physical fitness training. The jungles were thick with razor-sharp elephant grass. The rivers held bloodsucking leeches. Most dangerous of all, a thick canopy of rain forest covered the land and hid the movements of enemy soldiers.

Snipers routinely ambushed Powell's South Vietnamese unit, usually killing the men at the head of a column. There was never any warning. As the unit patrolled, everything would be calm. The only sounds came from birds high above in the canopy of the rain forest. Suddenly, the sound of gunfire would pierce the air. The South Vietnamese soldiers could never pinpoint the source of the shooting. By the time they took cover and positioned themselves to return fire, the shooting had stopped and the attackers were gone.

Powell saw men injured and killed by snipers for a couple of months. The situation frustrated and angered him. How could he fight an enemy that was almost invisible? Making matters worse, the enemy soldiers did not wear uniforms. They wore the same kinds of clothing as the local people and often blended in with the local villagers. It was difficult fighting an enemy that was hard to identify.

Powell thought the men could do more to protect themselves, so he suggested that Captain Hieu provide them with bulletproof vests. The Vietnamese officer listened politely each time his American adviser mentioned the idea. He didn't do anything about it, though. Finally, after repeated nagging, Hieu gave some of his men the protection. Hieu didn't think the vests would help much. But his opinion soon changed.

On a forest trail, the unit was ambushed. A soldier wearing a vest was struck in the chest by a bullet. The bullet knocked him down, but it did not kill him.

Powell pried the flattened bullet from the vest and showed it to the other soldiers. The man who had been hit stood in disbelief, glad to be alive. From that time forward, Hieu and his soldiers had more respect for their American adviser.

A few months into Powell's tour, his unit started collecting lumber to build a new base. To down the huge trees in the region, the Vietnamese soldiers preferred dynamite. But dynamite was in short supply and expensive, so Powell had a chain saw flown in. These troops had other ideas, however. To Powell's shock one day, he found them using machine gun fire to take down the trees. Such a waste of valuable ammunition was unthinkable to Powell.

Powell waited for the proper moment, then quietly explained to Captain Hieu that the bullets his men used cost eight cents apiece. The officer estimated the number of bullets it would take to fell one large tree. He then thought about the number of trees they had already cut. As he thought and added, the waste of money staggered him. He immediately ordered his men to use saws instead of bullets to cut the trees.

Powell could have given the soldiers an army-style chewing out. He could have simply told Hieu that the actions of his troops were wrong. But Powell was learning to be a diplomat. Rather than bark orders and criticisms, he gave Captain Hieu the facts he needed to make his own decision.

THE HOME STRETCH

Late in July, Powell suffered a wound that took him out of the combat zone. While on patrol with his unit, he stepped into a *punji* trap. This was a simple booby trap made by placing sharpened stakes, with the points up, into a concealed hole. The tips were usually covered with animal dung, which would badly infect any wound the trap might cause.

The wound to Powell's foot was not life threatening. It was, however, serious enough for a trip back to Saigon and a Purple Heart (the medal awarded to soldiers wounded in combat). In Saigon the wound was treated, and Powell recovered with no complications. Since he was very close to the end of his tour, he did not return to the front lines after the injury. He spent the last weeks at headquarters before shipping out to the United States.

Powell headed to Birmingham, to Alma's parents' house. He was happy to be going home, and he was glad to leave the fighting in Southeast Asia. But he was also excited for another reason. During his absence, Alma had given birth to their first child, a son named Michael. Eight months old when his father arrived in Birmingham, Michael reacted coolly to the strange man he had never seen. But soon father and son bonded, and Powell settled into his new family life.

Segregated public drinking fountains. When Powell returned to the United States, Jim Crow laws, which mandated separate facilities for blacks and whites, were still widely enforced.

Chapter **FOUR**

THE HOME FRONT

UPON RETURNING HOME TO THE UNITED STATES, Colin Powell found himself in the midst of another sort of war zone. For generations the American South had been segregated. Blacks couldn't attend school with whites. They weren't allowed in many restaurants and stores. They couldn't live in white neighborhoods. In southern cities, drinking fountains were designated "whites only" and "colored only." Interracial marriages were banned. During elections blacks were often forcibly kept from voting.

But during the 1950s and early 1960s, the Civil Rights movement had gone into high gear. Leaders such as the Reverend Martin Luther King Jr. were challenging segregation and demanding equality for black people.

They wanted integration—the free association of all races—in schools, neighborhoods, and businesses. The Civil Rights protesters used nonviolent methods. They held peaceful demonstrations and marches. But these peaceful protests were often met with a violent response. The whites who opposed integration sometimes bombed black homes and churches, lynched and shot some protesters, and beat and threatened many others.

Martin Luther King Jr., front row, second from left, *and other activists peacefully march to demand civil rights for all.*

One of the most volatile cities was Birmingham, Alabama, where Alma lived with her parents and had given birth to Michael. While Colin was in Vietnam, the city had exploded into violence. In early 1963, Martin Luther King Jr. had led a series of nonviolent protests in Birmingham. In response, the white police chief, Bull Connor, had turned attack dogs and powerful water hoses on the demonstrators, many of them teenagers. Later in the year, a bomb exploded inside the Sixteenth Street Baptist Church, killing four black girls.

The violence hit close to home. Alma had often attended events at the Sixteenth Street Baptist Church. She and her family knew many of King's young demonstrators. One day as she was hanging Michael's diapers on the line, she heard gunshots not far from home. A white sniper had tried to kill a neighbor.

Alma was frightened by the violence, but it did not surprise her. She had grown up in Birmingham and was used to the racial hatred there. She knew that she couldn't go freely into certain bowling alleys or lunch counters. If she wanted to eat in a restaurant or stay in a hotel, she had to find one owned by blacks or one designated as open to black customers.

Colin hadn't experienced much discrimination growing up in New York City. But he was far from naive about racial prejudice. He recalled how the bars in Fort Benning, Georgia, had refused to serve him. He was upset to hear about the violence that had raged so close to his wife and baby son while he was in Vietnam.

And it angered him to think that while he was serving his country, his country did little to secure the rights and safety of his own people. "Because of my position and the things I was doing in my career... I didn't have a chance to participate in [the Civil Rights] struggle in an active way," he later recalled. "But you better believe that I identified with that struggle."

FAMILY TIME

Colin's next assignment took him back to Fort Benning, Georgia, the site of his basic, airborne, and Ranger training. In terms of race relations, the Fort Benning area was no better than Birmingham, Alabama. This fact

Powell, second from left, *runs as part of his officer training.*

became obvious as soon as the Powells started looking for a place to live. The other officers lived in all-
white neighborhoods, but the Powells were not
welcome in these parts of the city. Eventually, they
rented a house in Phenix City, a black community
just over the Alabama border.

In Columbus, the nearest town to Fort Benning,
Colin sometimes heard racial slurs on the streets. One
day at a restaurant, Buck's Barbeque, a waitress eyed
Powell curiously. Was he Puerto Rican? she wondered.
When Powell replied that he was African American,
the waitress explained that she couldn't serve him. If
he wanted a hamburger, he'd have to pick it up at the
back door. Powell promptly left the restaurant.

On the base, however, Colin was warmly accepted
by his fellow soldiers. He did a variety of work and
study at Fort Benning. First he tested new equipment
used by soldiers: rifles, pistols, even socks and rain-
coats. He also took the Pathfinder course, which con-
sisted of elite paratrooper training. In August 1964,
he began the Infantry Officers Advanced Course,
where captains were trained to become company
commanders.

Officers enrolled in the course were provided with
family housing, so the Powells moved from Phenix
City onto the base. Overall, Fort Benning was a good
place to raise a family, and Colin and Alma added to
theirs in 1965. That's when Linda Powell was born on
April 16 at a Fort Benning army hospital.

Powell continued to advance steadily in his career. In May 1966, he was promoted to the rank of major. A year later, he entered the Army Command and General Staff College at Fort Leavenworth, Kansas. This yearlong training program for majors and lieutenant colonels was highly selective, and it was an honor to be admitted. Although moving to Kansas brought the stresses of packing and unpacking, it was a small inconvenience for Powell and his family. Overall, army life treated Colin Powell well, and he lived up to its challenges. At Fort Leavenworth, he graduated second in his class out of a total of 1,244 officers.

A REAL WAR

Shortly before the Powells moved to Kansas, Colin received a phone call from an old Pershing Rifle buddy. It was bad news: Tony Mavroudis, Colin's dear friend from college, had been killed in combat in Vietnam. Colin was very sad to hear of his friend's death, but he wasn't shocked. By then American soldiers were dying by the thousands in Vietnam.

By the late 1960s, the United States had been in Vietnam for ten years. But the Americans were no longer just advisers in the conflict. By then they were fully part of the fight. The United States had sent about half a million troops into combat. It had dropped thousands of bombs on the enemy. Yet it seemed to be no closer to defeating the communists than it had been during Powell's first tour.

Powell was disturbed by the situation in Vietnam. The war appeared to be unwinnable, yet U.S. leaders were not willing to admit defeat. What's more, the U.S. soldiers did not have a clear sense of why they were fighting, nor did the American public. As more and more American troops were killed, people at home became increasingly alarmed. Many Americans, especially college students, protested against the war, demanding that it be stopped. Many young men refused to fight.

Veterans and other U.S. citizens protest the war in Vietnam outside the White House in Washington, D.C.

Powell understood the arguments of the war resisters. In some ways he even agreed with them. But he had a job to do.

In mid-1968, his orders came down to report back to Vietnam. It would be yet another separation from his family—and another dangerous one. Alma and the kids moved back to Birmingham, where they shared a house with Alma's divorced sister and her children. Powell left the country on July 21.

Arriving in Saigon, Powell was surprised to see how much the country had changed since his first tour. The city's once elegant streets were clogged with army vehicles. When he stepped off the helicopter at Duc Pho, his battalion headquarters, he nearly tripped over crates of ammunition left rusting in haphazard piles. A stench hung in the air from the open latrines. The American soldiers were dirty, discouraged, and undisciplined.

Powell did not stay long at Duc Pho. He was quickly brought into the inner circle of commanders who helped plan the war in his sector. Based at Chu Lai, he served as a staff officer to Major General Charles M. Gettys, a division commander. Although stationed behind the combat troops, Powell and the rest of Gettys's staff were by no means out of danger there. Enemy attacks were common, even at headquarters. In Vietnam "there were no safe havens," reported one of Powell's colleagues.

In his job with Gettys, Powell spent a lot of time in helicopters, traveling from unit to unit. The terrain

Powell, right, *survived a helicopter crash in 1968. Powell bravely helped other passengers escape the burning helicopter.*

was mountainous and thick with trees. Landings could be treacherous. One day, November 16, 1968, a helicopter carrying Gettys, Powell, and several other officers crashed during a landing attempt in the mountains west of Chu Lai.

Powell escaped from the wreck but turned to see the helicopter on fire. The pilot and other officers were still trapped inside. Instantly, Powell rushed back to the wreckage. With the help of other soldiers on the ground, he pulled one man after another to safety. Back at the Chu Lai base hospital, X rays revealed that Powell had performed his heroics on a broken ankle. His actions earned him the Soldier's Medal, awarded for bravery in noncombat situations. The rest of his tour was far less dramatic. By July 1969, Powell was back home with his family.

The entrance to the Government Building at George Washington University. Powell enrolled in graduate school at the university in 1969.

Chapter **FIVE**

LESSONS IN LEADERSHIP

BEFORE LEAVING VIETNAM, POWELL HAD APPLIED TO a two-year graduate program at George Washington University (GWU) in Washington, D.C. Top-ranking officers had to have graduate degrees. If Powell wanted to keep advancing through the military ranks, he'd need one, too. Powell didn't get to choose his own course of study, however. The army wanted him to study business administration. And since the army was footing the bill, he went along with the idea. He arrived on the GWU campus in September 1969.

Powell enjoyed life at George Washington University. He liked the free exchange of ideas between students and professors. He enjoyed his classes in computer systems, data management, and business administration.

He was more focused and mature than he had been when he first went to college. This time he earned mostly As in his classes. Between his first and second year in the program, Powell was promoted to lieutenant colonel.

At home Powell took great pleasure in fatherhood and family life. The family bought a house in Woodbridge, Virginia, a suburb of Washington. A second daughter, Annemarie, was born there in May 1970. The Powells joined the local Episcopal church. Colin taught fifth graders at the church's Sunday school and helped with fund-raising and other church activities. Young Michael became an acolyte at the church, just as his father had done as a boy.

THE SEAT OF POWER

Powell graduated from GWU in 1971. His next stop was the Pentagon, headquarters for the Department of Defense. His official title was operations research analyst. After two years in graduate school, Powell looked forward to the discipline of army life. But at the Pentagon, he was surprised to discover a military establishment under siege. Complaints about American involvement in Vietnam echoed in nearly every newspaper in the land.

Military leaders could not help being affected. They thought about change—about making the military more efficient and effective. In one of Powell's first assignments at the Pentagon, he was asked to produce a report about cutting the size of the army from 1.6 million soldiers to just 500,000.

Powell did not stay long at that job. At the insistence of his superiors, he applied to become a White House fellow. The yearlong fellowship program was designed to develop future leaders. It involved hands-on work experience in the executive branch of government. After filling out lengthy applications and enduring more than three days of interviews, Powell was accepted to the program in mid-1972. He was one of just seventeen people accepted from a pool of more than a thousand applicants.

Because he had a business degree, Powell was assigned to the Office of Management and Budget.

Powell beat out thousands of other applicants to become a White House fellow in 1972.

Powell meets with President Richard Nixon. His White House fellowship put him in touch with powerful U.S. officials.

This quiet office was actually one of the most powerful in Washington. It controlled the spending of the other departments in government. Powell served as special assistant to the office's deputy director. In this job, he handled a number of special projects. But mostly he watched and learned. He saw the gears of government at work. He discussed presidential power with President Richard Nixon and laws with members of Congress. He met other young professionals starting their climb through the ranks of military and political power. In January 1973, Powell and the other fellows took a trip to the Soviet Union and Eastern Europe. Powell relished the chance to meet new people and hear new ideas along the way.

It was an exciting time. But in the end, Powell longed for the life of a soldier. He wanted to lead troops. In the spring of 1973, he asked the army for a command of his own. There was no guarantee he'd get one, since positions were based on availability and army politics—that is, favors and friendships often influenced who would be chosen. Powell wound up assigned to command an infantry battalion in South Korea.

Had he a choice, Powell would have preferred another assignment. It was an "unaccompanied tour," which meant his family could not come along. This would be his third separation from ten-year-old Michael, his second from eight-year-old Linda, and his first from three-year-old Annemarie. "In our house, when you were young, your mother was your primary parent," Michael Powell later recalled. "You were always very admiring of your father, but he worked a lot. He was on the job night and day; there was the Korea tour and Vietnam when he went away."

The Office of Management and Budget wanted Powell to stay another year. He and Alma considered the offer. But Colin knew that he would not advance further in the army if he stayed in Washington. D.C.

In some ways, the assignment in Korea was a sacrifice. But Colin and Alma decided it was the best career choice.

"Bro P"

Powell headed to South Korea in 1973. He was part of a force sent to maintain the 1953 truce between North Korea and South Korea, established at the end of the Korean War. This assignment would prove to be an important lesson for Powell in military leadership. His teacher would be his commanding officer, Major General Henry E. "the Gunfighter" Emerson.

Emerson was a tall, rugged man of about fifty. His intense gaze and hooked nose made him look like a bird of prey. From the first, Powell liked Emerson's incredible energy. When addressing his staff during meetings, Emerson was like a preacher. He always thundered to a close with the same phrase: "If we don't do our jobs right, soldiers won't win."

The United States had finally left Vietnam earlier that year—without a victory after more than a decade of armed struggle. The conflict had left the military demoralized, especially the enlisted men. This attitude was evident in Korea. Many of the soldiers in Powell's battalion came from poor neighborhoods. Many were black. Most hadn't volunteered for the army—they had been drafted. Overall, the soldiers lacked discipline and distrusted authority. Many soldiers abused drugs. Racial tensions were high. But General Emerson was

Powell stops to pose for a photograph in 1974 during his tour in South Korea.

committed to improving morale among the troops. He found a kindred spirit in Lieutenant Colonel Powell.

Powell proved to have a cool hand in dealing with the tensions on base, as illustrated by one encounter with a young black soldier near a company recreation room. The man was out of control. His eyes were fire red, and he held a pool cue like a club. Powell could tell that the soldier was either drunk or drugged.

"Somebody's gonna die!" the soldier bellowed. "You put my buddy in jail. Nobody's gonna put me in jail. Somebody's gonna die first!"

Powell weighed his options. The military police had been contacted. He could wait and let them wrestle the man to the ground and carry him away in chains. But Powell thought there might be another, more dignified way. He stepped forward. He addressed the soldier in a gentle voice:

"Son, put the cue down."

"No, Sir."

"Do you know who I am?"

"Yes, Sir, Colonel Powell."

Powell came closer. He continued in a calm, quiet voice: "I want you to put the cue down before you hurt somebody. I want you to put it down before somebody hurts you. You see, if you don't do what I tell you, all these men are going to [beat] you. Then, when they're done, you're going to the stockade for a year. What sense does that make? So put the cue down, and we'll have a nice talk."

Suddenly, the man dropped the cue and broke down in tears. The confrontation was over. He was placed on restriction for several weeks and soon was back on regular duty. Powell passed the reformed soldier one day and heard him remark to his buddies: "That's Bro P, Brother Powell, he's all right."

Powell's actions had kept the soldier from serious punishment. Powell had not only salvaged the man's military life, but he had also salvaged a good soldier for the military. The fact that the young man was black was certainly a source of pride for Powell.

In turn, "Bro P" was beloved by the black troops. But he never forgot his duty as an army officer. When the situation demanded it, Powell could be very strict. Years later he wrote in his autobiography:

> Among the blacks, I had some of the finest soldiers and NCOs [noncommissioned officers] I have ever known. They had found in the army a freedom in which they could fulfill themselves. I did not like seeing their proud performance tarnished by nihilistic [destructive] types, a minority within a minority. What problem soldiers needed, like the kid with the pool cue, was someone to care about them.... I wanted to care for them positively.

At the end of the yearlong tour, Powell found that he had grown as an officer. He had always been efficient. But now he had a deeper understanding of how to motivate the soldiers in his command. General Emerson recognized that Powell had the ability to be a top commander. In fact, Emerson recommended Powell as general material, remarking, "He really raised the morale, especially the [spirit] of that unit. It came from very low to very high.... I put on his report that this guy should be a brigadier general as quick as the law allows." That recommendation would add steam to a career that was already moving fast.

President Nixon resigned in 1974 after the Watergate scandal.

Chapter **SIX**

STEPPING-STONES TO POWER

WITH THE RANK AND RECORD TO MAKE HIM THE envy of many older officers, Colin Powell returned to the United States in 1974. These were difficult times for the nation. Nearly sixty thousand American soldiers had died during the bloody Vietnam conflict. The long, controversial war had ended in defeat. It had left many Americans feeling betrayed by and mistrustful of government. In addition, President Nixon was forced to resign in 1974. His downfall came when it was revealed that his staff had carried out burglary, wiretapping (listening in on private telephone conversations), and other illegal activities meant to help Nixon win reelection. The events came to be called the Watergate scandal. Powell returned to Washington a month after Nixon resigned.

Powell had been selected to attend the National War College at Fort McNair in Washington, D.C.

The Powell family about 1975. Despite his busy schedule, Powell always found time for his family.

The college trains high-ranking officers from all branches of the armed forces, as well as employees of the Central Intelligence Agency, the State Department, and other government agencies. There are several other war colleges, but the National War College is considered the best. Only 140 slots were available each year, and Powell knew that his acceptance was a great honor.

He looked at his admission as a chance to further sharpen his skills. He began classes in the fall of 1975.

It was a good time to be at the college. Across the nation, college campuses were alive with fiery discussions and bold new thoughts. The War College was no exception. Questions swirled everywhere: What had gone wrong in Vietnam? What had gone wrong with Nixon's presidency? The country was looking inward and trying to plot a new course.

Powell loved the feel of college life again. He took courses in history, politics, diplomacy, and military theory. He studied the writings of a nineteenth-century Prussian army officer named Karl von Clausewitz. More than one hundred years earlier, in the book *On War*, Clausewitz had written: "No one starts a war, or rather no one in his senses should do so, without first being clear in his mind what he intends to achieve by that war and how he intends to achieve it." Powell reflected on this wisdom and realized that the United States had failed to heed it in Vietnam. He vowed to remember it.

Powell graduated from the National War College in 1976, confident that he was ready to lead the military into a new era. That year he was promoted to full colonel. His next assignment took him to Fort Campbell, Kentucky, where he commanded the Second Brigade of the 101st Airborne Division.

For this assignment the whole family could come along. The Powells sold their house outside Washington.

And they set out for Fort Campbell. The base was the family's home for the next fifteen months. There, the three kids attended schools on the base, and Alma kept busy with volunteer work. Colin also took up a new hobby at Fort Campbell—fixing cars. He had learned some basics from a neighbor in Washington. By the time he reached Fort Campbell, he was doing minor repair work on the family car—an old Chrysler that had cost him fifty dollars.

IN AND OUT OF WASHINGTON

By 1977 Powell was back in the nation's capital. By this time, Jimmy Carter was president of the United States. Powell had been offered a job in Carter's government: special assistant to the deputy secretary of defense, based at the Pentagon. Once again Powell would have preferred to stay in the field. But army leaders made it clear that they wanted him in Washington.

So the family packed up and moved once more. They settled in Burke Center, Virginia. Not long afterward, in early 1978, the family received some bad news. Luther Powell, Colin's father, had been diagnosed with cancer of the liver. Several months later, he died.

It was a period of sadness for the Powell family, but for Colin there was little time for mourning. In his job at the Pentagon he worked in the nerve center of the American military. He often worked twelve-hour days. But the whole family took time to celebrate when Powell was promoted to brigadier general in 1979.

(Generals in the U.S. Army advance through four levels. Brigadier general is the first level. With each promotion, the general wears another star on his or her shoulder.) His mother, Arie, as well as many relatives, came to Washington for the formal ceremony held on June 1. Colin himself was filled with pride. His only disappointment that day was that his father had not lived to see his promotion.

Promotions—both military and civilian—came fast and furious from then on. Toward the end of the Carter Administration, Powell moved from the Defense Department to the Energy Department. Then, after Ronald Reagan became president in 1980, Powell commanded infantry divisions in Colorado and Kansas. These assignments enabled him to move even higher in the military ranks—he became a major general (two stars).

He then returned to Washington to become senior military assistant to Caspar Weinberger, secretary of defense in the Reagan administration. In this position, Powell was involved in key military decisions in a variety of international hot spots, including Grenada, Lebanon, Nicaragua, and Libya. Every step of the way, through every crisis and decision, Powell's talents were evident. In meetings "Powell usually silenced the opposition unless the opposition was very well versed in the subject," said one Reagan official. "People were afraid to challenge him because they felt he knew more than they did."

As hardworking as he was, Powell still made time to relax. At home he continued to work on cars. By then he had become a skilled mechanic. He specialized in old Volvos, a Swedish make of automobile. He loved to restore the cars and resell them, often to friends. He liked listening to music, including jazz greats Benny Goodman, Louis Armstrong, and Count Basie. He also watched his children—by then teenagers—grow and develop their own interests. Linda took up acting. Annemarie liked ice-skating and cheerleading.

Michael, the oldest of the children, seemed destined to follow in his father's footsteps. After graduating from high school in Burke Center, Michael attended the College of William and Mary, an elite university in Williamsburg, Virginia. Like his father, Michael joined Army ROTC during college. After graduation in 1985, he entered the army as a second lieutenant—just as his father had done. After basic training, he became platoon leader of an armored cavalry unit in West Germany, near the Czechoslovakian border. The night before Michael shipped out, Powell offered him some advice. He told Michael to take care of himself—and to take care of his soldiers.

Colin Powell also lived in Germany again briefly. In 1986 he spent five months in charge of the Fifth Corps in Frankfurt—with seventy-five thousand soldiers under his command. He then returned to Washington to serve as deputy to National Security Adviser Frank Carlucci, head of the National Security

Council (NSC). By then Powell was a lieutenant general (three stars).

The National Security Council advises the president on matters of defense, foreign policy, and intelligence. When Powell arrived at the NSC, the council was watching closely as dramatic changes began to take place in the government of the Soviet Union. This enemy nation, long run by communist dictators, began to extend more freedom to its people. Powell and the other NSC leaders were pleased by the changes, but they still watched their old enemy with suspicion.

National Security Council member Colin Powell briefs President Ronald Reagan.

Powell also helped the NSC reorganize and restore its reputation after the Iran-Contra affair, a scandal involving the government's secret shipment of arms to Iran. Powell was called to testify before Congress about the scandal. Although he had known about the operation, he was never accused of any wrongdoing in the matter.

TRAGEDY HITS HOME

On June 27, 1987, Powell was at his desk at the NSC when an urgent call came in from Germany. His son, Michael, had been critically injured in a jeep accident, along with two other soldiers. Colin and Alma flew to Germany immediately. They found their son in intensive care in an army hospital. His injuries were massive. He was flown to Walter Reed Army Medical Center in Washington, D.C. He lived there for roughly the next year, undergoing multiple surgeries, physical therapy, and painful rehabilitation. His parents and sisters spent every spare minute by his side. Michael's recovery was slow and difficult, but he gradually regained most of his strength and health.

Powell spent as much time with Michael as he could, but his career took most of his energy. In November 1987, Frank Carlucci was named secretary of defense, and Powell took over the top spot at the NSC. With this promotion, he became the nation's first black national security adviser. A year later, George H. W. Bush won the presidential election.

He asked Powell to stay on in his administration, and the position was a big one: chairman of the Joint Chiefs of Staff.

TOP JOB

The Joint Chiefs of Staff (JCS) is made up of the chairman, plus the head commanders of the army, navy, marines, and air force. The chiefs advise the president on military matters. In wartime the chairman commands the armed forces in collaboration with the president and the secretary of defense. The chairman outranks all other officers on the JCS. Thus, he is the highest-ranking military officer in the nation.

Powell's appointment as chairman of the JCS was a historic moment. At age fifty-two, he was the youngest chairman ever. He was also the first African American to get the job and the only chairman who had not earned his undergraduate degree at an official military college such as the U.S. Military Academy or the U.S. Naval Academy. What's more, President Bush had passed over several more experienced officers to make the choice. But Powell was well prepared for the job. He had years of experience and a gift for working with others. He understood politics as well as anyone in government.

Before officially becoming chairman in October 1989, Powell briefly served as commander in chief of Forces Command—head of all U.S-based army personnel in the nation (and a prerequisite for the JCS job).

As chairman of the Joint Chiefs of Staff, General Powell was President George Bush's top military adviser.

He also earned his fourth star—along with the simple title "general."

On the job, the challenges came quickly. First, in late 1989, the United States invaded Panama, a small nation in Central America. The action was taken to overthrow the country's leader, General Manuel Noriega, who was charged with allowing drugs to pass through Panama to the United States. The invasion was brief and successful. Other military actions took place in Somalia, Bosnia, El Salvador, and the Philippines.

The next year, the communist Soviet Union collapsed and broke into a number of independent states. Suddenly, the Cold War—the hostility between the United States and the Soviet Union—was over. The biggest American enemy for almost fifty years was no longer a military threat. As a result, Americans demanded a reduction in military spending. Congress responded to the call by proposing cuts in the military budget. As chairman of the JCS, Powell had to make sure the cuts did not weaken the armed forces. Instead, he moved to create a leaner, more efficient military.

Had Powell simply helped downsize the military, his chairmanship of the JCS may have been memorable but not historic. But we remember soldiers for the wars they fight—and Colin Powell was about to make his place in history.

Generals Colin Powell, seated, left, *and Norman Schwarzkopf,* seated, right, *with Secretary of Defense Richard Cheney,* seated center, *and members of the Joint Chiefs of Staff.*

Chapter SEVEN

CENTER OF THE STORM

WHEN POWELL WAS APPOINTED CHAIRMAN OF THE Joint Chiefs of Staff, he was well known in Washington circles. But most ordinary Americans had never heard of General Colin Powell. That was about to change. War was brewing halfway around the world in the Middle Eastern nation of Iraq, and Chairman Colin Powell would soon be at the center of it.

Early on the morning of August 2, 1990, eighty thousand Iraqi troops crossed the border into the small, oil-rich nation of Kuwait, located on the Persian Gulf. The invasion came after decades of disputes between the two countries. President Saddam Hussein, Iraq's dictator, had ordered the attack, claiming Kuwait was Iraqi territory.

Powell, left center, *and members of President George Bush's cabinet discuss U.S. responses to Iraq's invasion of Kuwait in 1990.*

No other governments recognized the claim, and the United Nations (UN) demanded that Iraq remove its forces from its neighbor's soil. Hussein would not budge, claiming that Kuwait had wrongly been separated from his country when European powers created new national boundaries in the Middle East after World War I (1914–1918). As the world watched, Hussein's invading forces took full control of the tiny neighboring nation.

International leaders, particularly those from other Middle Eastern countries, tried to talk Hussein into releasing the territory he had seized. He stubbornly refused. So the leaders tried another tack. The United Nations declared an economic boycott. Countries were instructed not to do business with Iraq. By cutting off trade, the UN hoped to hurt the Iraqi economy and pressure Hussein to pull his troops out of Kuwait.

The United States Acts

Colin Powell and the other U.S. leaders watched the situation in Iraq and Kuwait closely. Like many people, Powell hoped the economic boycott would work. If it did not, the United States planned to use military force against Hussein. Despite diplomatic talks, positions on both sides continued to harden. Hussein showed no sign of backing down. Finally, on November 29 the United Nations set a deadline: If Iraq did not withdraw from Kuwait by January 15, 1991, the UN would authorize its member nations to attack the Iraqis.

President Bush instructed Powell to create a plan for attacking Iraq. The attack would include U.S. forces and troops from France, Great Britain, Egypt, Syria, and other countries. The United States was expected to take the lead if and when fighting began. That would put young American men and women in danger. And that was not something Colin Powell would do without a great amount of thought. American lives were too important. It was a lesson learned from Vietnam— one that he would never forget. "War is a deadly game," Powell wrote in his autobiography, "and I do not believe in spending the lives of Americans lightly."

Powell spent much of the fall of 1990 helping members of Congress understand the situation in the Persian Gulf. The task was not easy. As Americans watched the buildup of forces in the gulf, fears of another Vietnam War surfaced. What if U.S. forces found themselves stuck in another drawn-out war they could not win? many wondered. Like Powell, Congress and the public also worried about the loss of American lives in the course of the fighting.

But Powell took care to speak to every fear. In the end, he helped convince Congress that the use of overwhelming force would most likely bring the war to a swift conclusion with little loss of American life. On January 12, 1991, Congress approved the use of American troops in the Persian Gulf. The offensive plan was called Operation Desert Storm.

The January 15 deadline for Hussein to pull back his forces came and went. Iraq's troops remained in Kuwait. On January 17, 1991, the allied attack began. Powell oversaw the operation from Washington, while army General Norman Schwarzkopf commanded the troops in the field. "Our strategy for going after [the Iraqi] army is very, very simple." Powell told reporters a few days after the fighting began. "First we are going to cut it off. And then we are going to kill it."

The allies started with an air attack. For more than a month, allied aircraft bombed Iraqi bridges, artillery, and troops. Most of Iraq's planes were grounded or destroyed. Most of its supply depots lay in ruin.

General Powell thanks and supports troops during the Persian Gulf War. Powell's genuine concern for soldiers earned him their deep respect.

With the enemy reeling from the air attacks, ground forces moved in on February 24. Allied troops closed in on the Iraqi forces remaining in Kuwait. On February 27, the allies reclaimed the capital of Kuwait City. By February 28, Iraqi forces had been completely pushed out of Kuwait. The war was over. In the end, the United States decided not to destroy Saddam Hussein's government, but his army was all but wiped out. His nation seemed to be thoroughly defeated.

Operation Desert Storm was a stunning success. With it, the United States had thrown off the embarrassment of the Vietnam War. And Colin Powell had stepped into the history books and into the limelight. He won high praise for his cool-headed handling of the conflict, with few American lives lost.

He was admired for the thoughtful way he had sent young men and women into battle. He came to be known as a soldier who cared. And Colin Powell was a celebrity. His face graced news reports and magazine covers. The National Association for the Advancement of Colored People gave him a prestigious honor—the Spingarn Medal, given annually to a black American who achieves at the highest level in his or her field.

TIME TO STEP DOWN

Despite all the acclaim, Powell simply went back to work after the war. Bill Clinton entered the presidency in 1992, and Powell stayed on in Clinton's administration. He became embroiled in the controversy over whether or not gays should be allowed to serve in the military, an issue that was never fully resolved. Troubles continued to simmer in hot spots such as Bosnia and Somalia. Powell attended to these issues with his usual diplomacy and diligence.

But by 1993, Powell had had enough of political life. He decided it was time to retire. At a formal ceremony in September, family and old friends gathered to honor Powell's thirty-five years of dedication to the U.S. military and the government. President Clinton presented Powell with a special going-away present: a rusty 1966 Volvo.

After thirty-five years of hard work, what would Colin Powell do next? He had many ideas. He could fix up Volvos. He could travel with Alma and spend

G.I. COLIN

When Colin Powell was a boy, he liked playing with toy soldiers. He certainly never imagined that someday kids would be playing with toy soldiers that looked like him! But in the 1990s, Hasbro Inc., the company that makes G.I. Joe action figures, added a Colin Powell doll to its "Historic Commanders" lineup. The Colin Powell G.I. Joe joined action figures modeled on Teddy Roosevelt, Dwight Eisenhower, George Patton, and other famous commanders from America's past. The toy came complete with an army uniform, insignias, flags, and dog tags.

time with his kids and his first grandchild, Michael's son Jeffrey. But Powell was too famous to just fade into the background. Many people were interested in his story of success. So Powell decided to sit down and write his autobiography, *My American Journey*. Published in 1995, it became an immediate bestseller. Powell toured the country to promote the book.

He found himself in great demand. Companies wanted him to speak at their meetings and conferences, and some would pay as much as seventy thousand dollars for one speech. He was asked to work with many nonprofit and educational organizations. He accepted several of these offers, joining the board of directors of the United Negro College Fund, the board of trustees at Howard University, an elite all-black college, and the board of governors of the Boys and Girls Clubs of America.

He enjoyed speaking to young people, especially young African Americans, with a message of hope. He explained to a reporter, "I've made myself very accessible to the Black press, and I do that as a way of just showing people, 'Hey, look at that dude. He came out of the South Bronx. If he got out, why can't I?'"

With all this acclaim and success, many people thought that Powell would make a great U.S. president.

Like many Americans, this man wanted Powell to run for president. Powell's leadership skills and strength of character appealed to voters across racial and political boundaries.

Powell, with his wife, Alma, announces to the press that he will not run for president in 1996.

In magazine surveys, he was consistently named one of the most admired people in the nation. He had never held elected office, yet polls showed that he would be a front-runner in the 1996 presidential election. Political leaders urged him to put his name forward. Rumors circulated that he would run. Powell considered the idea. But in the end, he decided not to pursue the office. In a press conference on November 8, 1995, he explained that he did not have the passion and commitment needed to run the race or do the job. The announcement shocked some people and saddened others. No doubt, potential rivals sighed in relief.

AMERICA'S PROMISE

Offers continued to pour in from schools and businesses, asking for Powell's involvement, but he turned down more offers than he accepted. Then he heard about a project that grabbed his attention. President Clinton, along with former Presidents George H. W. Bush, Jimmy Carter, and Gerald Ford and former First Lady Nancy Reagan were planning a three-day event in Philadelphia called the Presidents' Summit for America's Future. The summit would bring together governors, mayors, business leaders, and community organizers and would focus on ways to help America's youth.

Powell said the project "fit with my priorities. . . . I had said no to offers to chair studies [about problems facing American youth], to sit on boards to examine the cities. I wanted concrete goals, a focus on kids, deliverable results and a way to continue beyond the summit." So Powell agreed to get involved not only with the summit but also with a permanent organization that would carry on the work that the summit began. The organization was called America's Promise, and Powell became its founding chairman.

In this job, he worked tirelessly with a variety of leaders and community groups. He wrote a monthly column for the organization's website. He encouraged adults to become mentors for young people. He helped set up educational and job-training programs. He also encouraged young people to give back to their communities through volunteer work. "Most young people who have helped tell me that they get as much back from serving others as they give," Powell wrote. "Serving makes you feel good about yourself while you are making a difference in someone else's life. More than that, giving back improves your self-confidence and self-esteem, gives you a chance to learn new skills, and allows you to be a leader at an early age. Some young men and women have discovered talents they never knew they had and have even found their life's work through serving others."

General Powell stayed with America's Promise until 2000. Then another offer came along—an offer he couldn't refuse.

Colin Powell talks with a youngster during an event sponsored by America's Promise. Powell was the founding chairperson of the community service organization.

As secretary of state, Powell is at the center of world affairs.

Chapter EIGHT

POWELL, PEACE, AND WAR

COLIN POWELL HAD WORKED FOR THIRTY-FIVE YEARS as a warrior. He had commanded troops in Germany, Vietnam, and South Korea. He had earned the highest rank possible in the U.S. Army. He had overseen Operation Desert Storm brilliantly and ensured its swift success. But Colin Powell was far from warlike. He was friendly, soft-spoken, and diplomatic. He grieved for the thousands of young lives lost in Vietnam and vowed that during his leadership the United States would never again wage war without a clear sense of purpose. In short, Powell was as much a peacemaker as he was a warrior. When President George W. Bush, son of former president George Bush, took office in 2001, he recognized the peace-loving qualities in Powell.

President George W. Bush announces his appointment of Colin Powell to the cabinet position of secretary of state.

President Bush asked Powell to serve as the chief diplomat in his new administration. The job was secretary of state.

Colin Powell had been retired from government for almost ten years. Still, he did not hesitate to accept Bush's offer. He considered it an honor to serve his country. He was also pleased to be working alongside a number of talented individuals in Bush's new government. Dick Cheney, who had served as secretary of defense during the first Bush administration, would be Bush's vice president. Donald Rumsfeld, the new secretary of defense, had previously served as secretary of defense and White House chief of staff for

President Gerald Ford in the mid-1970s. He had also worked in the Reagan administration. Powell also knew Rumsfeld well from their many years in Washington. Condoleezza Rice, previously a professor of political science at Stanford University, took on the job of Bush's national security adviser. After Powell, she was only the second African American to ever hold this position.

As secretary of state, Powell would head the state department, the executive office that deals with U.S. foreign relations. The secretary advises the president on international affairs, serves on the National Security Council, and belongs to the president's cabinet. At his confirmation hearing held in front of the Senate Foreign Relations Committee on January 17, 2001, Powell acknowledged that his job would not be an easy one. He discussed many nations around the world—both friendly and unfriendly—and examined how the United States could improve its relations with those nations.

Powell identified the Middle East, particularly Iraq, as a critical area of concern. "This is the 10th year anniversary of the beginning of Desert Storm," he told the senators, "a war we wish we didn't have to fight. We wish the Iraqi leaders and their people had come to their senses back then, and not caused this conflict to happen. But it did happen. And we went into that war with clear political objectives, and those objectives were to kick the Iraqi army out of Kuwait; and they're gone. . . .

Unfortunately, Saddam Hussein is still in power. . . . Instead of seeking peace and prosperity for his people, we see a weakened Iraq that utters threats and pursues horrible weapons to terrorize its neighbors." Powell spoke with eloquence and authority about the Iraqi situation and others. It was clear to every senator in attendance that he was the right person to be the secretary of state. His confirmation was unanimous.

ATTACK ON AMERICA

At age sixty-three, Colin Powell was back at work at the highest level of government. His job took him around the world. Between February and September 2001, he traveled more than 110,000 miles and visited more than thirty countries. He met with prime ministers, presidents, and monarchs. He was rarely at home. Alma accompanied him on only one trip that year.

On September 11, 2001, Powell was in Lima, Peru, meeting with that nation's president, when aides handed him a series of notes. The news was shocking: hijackers had flown commercial airplanes into the Pentagon just outside Washington, D.C., and the World Trade Center towers in New York. Both cities were in turmoil. Thousands had been killed. Another hijacked plane had crashed in Pennsylvania, killing everyone onboard. The United States had been attacked by unknown terrorists. Powell immediately flew back to Washington.

A solemn Secretary of State Powell quickly leaves a meeting in Lima, Peru, to return to the United States. Only moments before, Powell had learned of the September 11 terrorist attacks.

Over the difficult days and weeks that followed, Powell attended lengthy meetings with President Bush and other top government officials. He spoke with the press eight times on September 12 alone. As the nation tried to come to grips with the tragedy, it became clear that a terrorist network named al-Qaeda had been responsible for the attacks. President Bush and his advisers began to formulate a plan to retaliate.

Shortly after the attacks, Powell addressed the Senate Foreign Relations Committee. "[President Bush] knew right away that he not only had to go after the perpetrators of these terrible attacks against us; he knew also that we had to go after terrorism," Powell explained.

"It wouldn't be enough just to deal with these perpetrators, who were soon identified as the al-Qaeda network. . . . [W]e had to undertake a campaign that goes
after terrorism in . . . its many forms around the world."

The U.S. military first moved into Afghanistan to
remove the Taliban, a regime that harbored many al-
Qaeda terrorists. In some ways, this action was conven-
tional, fought with guns, tanks, and bombs. But Powell
and other leaders realized that the "war on terrorism"
would be a war like no other. To succeed, the United
States would need to undermine the financial, techno-
logical, and communications networks of terrorist
groups. As Defense Secretary Donald Rumsfeld explained
to the *New York Times:* "Our response may include firing
cruise missiles into military targets somewhere in the
world; [but] we are just as likely to engage in electronic
combat to track and stop [terrorist] investments moving
through offshore banking centers. The uniforms of this
conflict will be bankers' pinstripes and [computer] pro-
grammers' [casual clothing] just as assuredly as desert
camouflage. . . . When we 'invade the enemy's territory,'
we may well be invading his cyberspace."

THE PEACEMAKER

As an experienced military man, Colin Powell was intri-
cately involved in the efforts to root out al-Qaeda members and other terrorists. But he was also the nation's
chief diplomat. As the United States tried to heal and
return to normal after the September 11 tragedy,

Powell meets with new Afghan leaders after the defeat of the Taliban in 2002.

Powell returned to the work of foreign diplomacy. He hit the road again, visiting nearly forty countries in nine months and logging nearing 140,000 miles in the process. He met with leaders in political trouble spots such as Afghanistan, Pakistan, and Israel. Everywhere he went, he brought a message of peace.

In late 2002, Powell once again turned his attention to the nation that had made him famous—Iraq, the U.S. enemy in Desert Storm—and its ruthless dictator, Saddam Hussein. Hussein had remained in power after the Persian Gulf War, and more than ten years later he appeared to be just as dangerous as ever. The international community suspected that he was producing nuclear, biological, and chemical weapons—

weapons that could kill vast numbers of people in a short time. Hussein routinely oppressed and terrorized ethnic groups within his own country, threatened neighboring nations, and railed against the United States and its allies. He even expressed support for the September 11 hijackers who had killed thousands of Americans. Some people suspected that he had offered support to al-Qaeda and other terrorist groups.

Finally, President George Bush declared that Hussein had to be removed from power. He worked hard in trying to rally Congress, the American public, and the United Nations to his cause. He wanted to attack Iraq if Saddam Hussein would not relinquish his "weapons of mass destruction." The world watched carefully as the president made his case for war.

Colin Powell had mixed feelings about going to war. "War should be the politics of last resort," he had written in his 1995 autobiography. "And when we go to war, we should have a purpose that our people understand and support; we should mobilize the country's resources to fulfill that mission and then go in to win. . . . Many of my generation, the career captains, majors, and lieutenant colonels seasoned in that war [Vietnam], vowed that when our turn came to call the shots, we would not quietly acquiesce in half-hearted warfare for half-baked reasons that the American people could not understand or support."

Because of this statement and others, Powell was viewed as something of a "dove"—an opponent of war—in the Bush administration. Nevertheless, he made it clear that when it came to Saddam Hussein, he agreed with President Bush. "Nobody wants war. . . , " he told TV talk show host Oprah Winfrey. "But do we want Saddam Hussein to have nuclear, chemical, and biological weapons that he can use . . . perhaps against us someday? This is the time to stop him."

But the world was not convinced that war was the right answer. Many members of the United Nations, including major U.S. allies such as France and Germany, opposed President Bush's call for invasion. Many world leaders preferred continuing with methods that were currently in progress, such as diplomatic talks, weapons inspections, and economic boycotts, to contain Iraq's power.

On February 5, 2003, Powell tried to persuade the UN Security Council that diplomacy and other peaceful efforts had failed and that military force against Iraq would be necessary. In a televised presentation, Powell outlined Iraq's history of brutality, deception, and defiance of international law. He showed satellite photos of Iraqi weapons facilities and played secret tape recordings of conversations between Iraqi military officers. He presented evidence of Iraq's chemical, biological, and nuclear weapons programs. He also showed alleged links between Iraq and the al-Qaeda terrorist network. At the end of his presentation, Powell made it clear that the United States was ready to take action.

He explained:

> We know that Saddam Hussein is determined to keep his weapons of mass destruction [and] is determined to make more. Given Saddam Hussein's history of aggression, . . . should we take the risk that he will not someday use these weapons . . . at a time when the world is in a much weaker position to respond?
>
> The United States will not and cannot run that risk for the American people. Leaving Saddam Hussein in possession of weapons of mass destruction for a few more months or years is not an option, not in a post-September 11th world.

Powell argues for the use of military force in Iraq before the UN Security Council in 2003.

The presentation left no doubt that the United States intended to go to war against Iraq, whether or not the rest of the United Nations was prepared to join the fight.

The war began on March 19, 2003. Although the United Nations did not ultimately back the effort, several countries did send troops to help the Americans. The U.S.-led coalition quickly defeated Iraqi defenses and moved into Baghdad, Iraq's capital city. The Americans then set about the tough job of rebuilding Iraq and setting up a new, democratic government in the nation.

As U.S. forces fought, Powell again traveled around the world, meeting with foreign leaders. He visited Turkey, Serbia, and Belgium in March and visited Northern Ireland in April.

In mid-May, with war in Iraq over, Powell planned a trip to the Middle Eastern nation of Saudi Arabia. Only hours before Powell's scheduled visit, suicide bombers attacked a housing compound in Riyadh, the Saudi capital. The compound was home to Americans and other Westerners. Thirty-four people were killed, including seven Americans. Nearly 200 people were injured.

The bombings appeared to be the work of the al-Qaeda network. Powell condemned the attacks as cowardly. He called them "a threat to the civilized world." It was clear that terrorism—and the war on it— showed no signs of slowing. What was clear was that in the face of an uncertain future, Americans were lucky to have Colin Powell—one of the nation's greatest warriors and greatest peacemakers—to lead them.

GLOSSARY

boycott: a refusal to do business with a government, person, or organization as a method of expressing disapproval or pressuring for change

communism: a political and economic system in which the government controls the economy, with no private property

discrimination: mistreatment of a person or group, usually based on racial or ethnic prejudice

integration: the mixing of different groups, such as blacks and whites, in schools, housing, and businesses

segregation: the separation of different groups, such as blacks and whites, in schools, housing, and businesses

SOURCES

11 Colin Powell and Joseph E. Persico, *My American Journey* (New York: Random House, 1995), 18.

13 Ibid., viii.

20 Ibid., 16.

21 Ibid., 13.

22 Howard Means, *Colin Powell: Soldier/Statesman, Statesman/Soldier* (New York: Ballantine Books, 1992), 43.

25 Ibid., 65.

28 Powell and Persico, *My American Journey,* 28.

28 Means, *Colin Powell,* 69.

30 Powell and Persico, *My American Journey,* 42.

31 Means, *Colin Powell,* 100–101.

50 Ibid., 120.

54 Ibid., 141.

61 David Roth, *Sacred Honor* (Grand Rapids, MI: Zondervan Publishing House, 1993), 105.

62 Powell and Persico, *My American Journey,* 180.

64 Ibid., 188–189.

65 Ibid., 192.

65 Means, *Colin Powell,* 166.

69 Quoted in Powell and Persico, *My American Journey,* 207.

71 Means, *Colin Powell,* 188.

81 Powell and Persico, *My American Journey,* 480.

82 Means, *Colin Powell,* 8.

86 "Powell, Colin (Luther)," *Biography.com,* 2000, <http://search.biography.com/print_record.pl?id=18549> (September 22, 2002).

88 Margaret Carlson, "The General's Next Campaign," *Time,* March 17, 1997, 28–29.

89 "General Powell's Corner," *America's Promise—The Alliance for Youth,* 2000, <http://www.americaspromise.org/GenPowellCorner/MTA.cfm> (September 22, 2002).

94 Colin Powell, "Confirmation Hearing by Colin L. Powell," *U.S. Department of State,* January 17, 2001, <http://www.state.gov/secretary/rm/2001/443.htm> (September 22, 2002).

96 "What Is a Hero," *Patriot Resource,* October 25, 2001, <http://www.patriotsource.com/wtc/federal/oct/011025/powell.html> (September 29, 2002).

96 "A New Kind of War," DefenseLINK U.S. *Department of Defense,* September 27, 2001, <http://www.defenselink.mil/speeches/2001/s20010927-secdef.html> (November 10, 2002).

98 Powell and Persico, *My American Journey,* 148–149.

99 "Interview on the Oprah Winfrey Show," *U.S. Department of State,* October 22, 2002, <http://www.state.gov/secretary/rm/2002/14563.htm> (November 10, 2002).

100 Colin Powell, "Remarks to the United Nations Security Council," *U.S. Department of State,* February 5, 2003, <http://www.state.gov/secretary/rm/2003/17300.htm> (April 23, 2003).

101 BBC News, "Saudi Bombing Deaths Rise," *BBC News World Edition,* May 13, 2003, <http://news.bbc.co.uk/2/hi/middle_east/3022473.stm> (May 23, 2003).

BIBLIOGRAPHY

BOOKS

Means, Howard. *Colin Powell: Soldier/Statesman, Statesman/Soldier.* New York: Ballantine Books, 1992.

Powell, Colin, and Joseph E. Persico. *My American Journey.* New York: Random House, 1995.

Roth, David. *Sacred Honor: A Biography of Colin Powell.* Grand Rapids, MI: Zondervan Publishing House, 1993.

Woodward, Bob. *The Commanders.* New York: Simon & Schuster, 1991.

WEBSITES

"Colin Powell," *San Diego 96, 1996,* <http://www.cnn.com/ALLPOLITICS/1996/conventions/san.diego/players/powell.bio> (October 19, 2002).

"Colin Powell: Secretary of State, United States of America," *The Hall of Public Service,* January 21, 2001, <http://www.achievement.org/autodoc/page/pow0pro-1> (September 22, 2002).

"General Powell's Corner," *America's Promise—The Alliance for Youth,* 2000, <http:www.americaspromise.org/GenPowellCorner/MTA.cfm> (September 22, 2002).

"Secretary of State Colin L. Powell," *U.S. Department of State,* 2002, <http://www.state/gov/secretary> (September 22, 2002).

FURTHER READING, VIDEOTAPES, AND WEBSITES

BOOKS

Finlayson, Reggie. *We Shall Overcome: The History of the American Civil Rights Movement.* Minneapolis: Lerner Publications Company, 2003.

Jones, Steven L. *The Red Tails: World War II's Tuskegee Airmen.* Logan, IA: Perfection Learning, 2001.

Levy, Debbie. *The Vietnam War.* Minneapolis: Lerner Publications Company, 2004.

Márquez, Herón. George W. Bush. Minneapolis: Lerner Publications Company, 2002.

Nardo, Don. *The War Against Iraq.* San Diego: Lucent Books, 2001.

Schraff, Anne. *Colin Powell: Soldier and Patriot.* Springfield, NJ: Enslow Publishers, 1997.

Sherman, Josepha. *The Cold War.* Minneapolis: Lerner Publications Company, 2004.

Taus-Bolstad, Stacy. *Iraq in Pictures.* Minneapolis: Lerner Publications Company, 2004.

———. *Vietnam in Pictures.* Minneapolis: Lerner Publications Company, 2003.

Wukovits, John. F. *Colin Powell.* San Diego: Lucent Books, 2000.

VIDEOTAPE

America's Black Warriors: Two Wars to Win (made-for-television documentary and videocassette). The History Channel/A&E Television Network, 2002.

Colin Powell: A Soldier's Campaign (made-for-television documentary and videocassette). ABC News Productions in association with A&E Networks, 2002.

WEBSITES

America's Promise—The Alliance for Youth
<http://www.americaspromise.org/>. Before serving as secretary of state, Colin Powell helped found America's Promise, an organization dedicated to improving the lives of American youth. This site examines the group's activities and tells how young people and adults can get involved in community service.

"Secretary of State Colin L. Powell," *U.S. Department of State,* 2002, <http://www.state/gov/secretary>. This site offers information on Colin Powell and his work at the State Department. It includes a special section on foreign affairs for young people.

The United States Army, <http://www.army.mil>. Colin Powell used the army as a stepping-stone to success. This site explains army organization, programs, and opportunities for soldiers.

INDEX

OTHER TITLES FROM LERNER AND A&E®:

Arthur Ashe
The Beatles
Benjamin Franklin
Bill Gates
Bruce Lee
Carl Sagan
Chief Crazy Horse
Christopher Reeve
Daring Pirate Women
Edgar Allan Poe
Eleanor Roosevelt
George Lucas
George W. Bush
Gloria Estefan
Jack London
Jacques Cousteau
Jane Austen
Jesse Owens
Jesse Ventura
Jimi Hendrix
John Glenn
Latin Sensations
Legends of Dracula
Legends of Santa Claus

Louisa May Alcott
Madeleine Albright
Malcolm X
Mark Twain
Maya Angelou
Mohandas Gandhi
Mother Teresa
Nelson Mandela
Oprah Winfrey
Osama bin Laden
Princess Diana
Queen Cleopatra
Queen Elizabeth I
Queen Latifah
Rosie O'Donnell
Saddam Hussein
Saint Joan of Arc
Thurgood Marshall
Tiger Woods
William Shakespeare
Wilma Rudolph
Women in Space
Women of the Wild West
Yasser Arafat

ABOUT THE AUTHOR

Reggie Finlayson holds a master's degree in journalism from Marquette University in Milwaukee, Wisconsin, and teaches at the Milwaukee Area Technical College. He is the author of many plays and several books for young readers that seek to preserve the history of African and African American people. His recent titles include *Nelson Mandela* and *We Shall Overcome: The History of the American Civil Rights Movement.*

PHOTO ACKNOWLEDGMENTS

The photographs are reproduced with the permission of: © AFP/CORBIS, pp. 2, 12, 92, 97, 100; Library of Congress, pp. 6, 9, 14, 22, 46, 56; © CORBIS SYGMA, pp. 10, 17, 18, 24, 27, 35, 36, 50, 55, 59, 60, 68, 78; © Bettmann/CORBIS, pp. 31, 41, 66; © CORBIS, pp. 40, 83; National Archives, p. 48; Theodore Hetzel/Swarthmore College Peace Collection, p. 53; Colin Powell's personal collection, p. 63; courtesy of the Ronald Reagan Presidential Library, p. 73; courtesy of the George H. W. Bush Presidential Library, pp. 76, 80; © Jacques M. Chenet/CORBIS, pp. 86, 87; © J. Allen Hansley/ZUMA Press, p. 89, © Reuters NewMedia Inc./CORBIS, pp. 90, 95.

Hard cover: front, © Chris Klenonis/ZUMA Press; back, courtesy of the United States Army
Soft cover: front, © ORJ/CORBIS SYGMA; back, courtesy of the United States Army